Help! My Spouse Committed Adultery

First Steps for
Dealing with Betrayal

Winston T. Smith

New
Growth
Press
www.newgrowthpress.com

All Scripture quotations, unless otherwise indicated, are
taken from the *Holy Bible,* New International Version®, NIV®.
Copyright © 1973, 1978, 1984 by International Bible Society.
Used by permission of Zondervan. All rights reserved.

New Growth Press, Greensboro, NC 27404
Copyright © 2008 by Christian Counseling & Educational
Foundation. All rights reserved. Published 2008

Cover Design: The DesignWorks Group, Nate Salciccioli and
Jeff Miller, www.thedesignworksgroup.com

Typesetting: Robin Black, www.blackbirdcreative.biz

ISBN-10: 1-934885-38-X
ISBN-13: 978-1-934885-38-3

Library of Congress Cataloging-in-Publication Data

Smith, Winston T., 1966-
  Help! my spouse committed adultery / Winston T. Smith.
    p. cm.
  Includes bibliographical references and index.
  ISBN 978-1-934885-38-3
  1. Adultery. 2. Christians—Sexual behavior. 3. Marriage—
Religious aspects—Christianity. I. Title.
  BV4627.A3S65 2008
  248.8′44—dc22

                              2008011937

Printed in Canada
20 19 18 17 16 15 14 13   10 11 12 13 14

Your spouse was unfaithful. Those four words don't do justice to the horror and pain you are experiencing. Betrayal takes your emotions all over the map. One moment you are burning with rage, next you are overwhelmed with fear, and then you just feel numb. These are all normal responses to the horror of betrayal.

Adultery Tears You Apart

In marriage two people become one. The Bible describes this as being "one flesh" (Genesis 2:24). Adultery tears apart the special intimacy and trust between a husband and a wife. That's why people say things like, "My heart has been torn out." Or, "I feel like I've been ripped apart."

You're probably also feeling shame. You feel weak, exposed, and embarrassed by what your spouse has done. You would do anything to cover it up and get rid of your awful feelings. You (or your friends) may even have some good sounding reasons for denying your feelings. You may think that because God is your refuge and strength you are denying your faith by expressing your pain. Or you may think your feelings move you away from the Christian goal of forgiveness. But it's a mistake to cover up or deny how you are feeling.

Give Voice to Your Betrayal

Don't be afraid to express what you are feeling. Let the words of David in Psalm 55 show you how to draw near to the Lord in the wake of betrayal:

> My heart is in anguish within me; the terrors of death assail me. Fear and trembling have beset me; horror has overwhelmed me....If an enemy were insulting me, I could endure it; if a foe were raising himself against me, I could hide from him. But it is you, a man like myself, my companion, my close friend.... My companion attacks his friends; he violates his covenant. His speech is smooth as butter, yet war is in his heart; his words are

4

more soothing than oil, yet they are drawn
swords. (Psalm 55:4–5, 12–13, 20–21)

David's honesty about his experience isn't a sign
of weakness or a denial of his faith; it's an *example*
of faith. Finding the words to express your pain is
important. It is a critical way for you to draw near
to God.

Expressing your pain to God allows you to
agree with him about the horrors of betrayal. All
sin is a form of betrayal. Our betrayal of God
is the reason Jesus had to go to the cross. Pain,
anger, horror, and disbelief are entirely appropriate responses to the things that grieve God. The
words of Psalm 55 are ultimately God's words
inspired by his Spirit. When you share your pain
with God, you are agreeing with him that betrayal
is an ugly sin.

Because Jesus experienced betrayal during his
time on earth, you are sharing your pain with someone who understands. He was rejected by family,

friends, and even his disciples. As you cry out, remember that Jesus' Spirit cries out in agreement with yours before God (Romans 8:26–27). Your cries are reaching an understanding and sympathetic ear. You are not alone. Of course, whether your marriage survives or not, you will have to forgive and let go of bitterness. But you can't forgive a wound you haven't acknowledged—you won't even know what you have to forgive. You are laying a foundation for forgiveness by being honest about how you've been wounded.

Adultery Is Forgivable

As awful as adultery is, it is forgivable. If you have just found out that your spouse has committed adultery, you're probably not in a position to forgive just yet. Your spouse may not have made a clean break from the other relationship, and you are caught up in a storm of reactions and feelings. But you need to know that it is possible for your spouse to truly be sorrowful and repentant and to change, and it *is* possible for you to truly forgive.

Right now you are probably thinking, *I could never trust him or her again.* Or, *I'll never be able to get images of them together out of my head.* These are completely understandable reactions to the horror of adultery. But unchallenged, these beliefs will inevitably lead you down the path toward bitterness and divorce.

Trust God to Protect You

There are a few things about forgiveness that you need to keep in mind to avoid being locked into bitterness and its consequences. First of all, forgiveness rests on a decision to trust God. You need to trust God to care for you and heal you. You need to trust God to protect you from betrayal and its effects. Often our sense that we can't forgive is rooted in self-protection. But self-protection isn't a good foundation for any relationship. It won't help you build a good relationship with God or your spouse. Instead, God calls you to faith. Trust God to protect and comfort you. Let the hurt and betrayal you have experienced from your spouse drive you closer to your faithful and trustworthy God. He will never disappoint you.

Psalm 91:2 says, "I will say of the Lord, 'He is my refuge and my fortress, my God, in whom I trust.'" Use this psalm as your prayer. Whenever you feel overcome by hurt and betrayal, cry out to God, asking him to be your refuge. He will answer you and help you.

Trust God for Your Spouse

You must also trust God to work in the heart of your spouse in his time. It is tempting to hold on tightly to your hurt and try to make your spouse suffer as much as you are. Sometimes being hurt becomes a justification for lashing out or withdrawing. When you do this, you are using self-protection to get back at your spouse. Instead of insisting on punishing your spouse, trust God to discipline and restore your spouse as he sees fit.

Forgiveness Is a Process

Even as you decide to trust God, your own emotions may urge you to take matters into your own hands. You might be tempted to nurture hateful thoughts, wallow in self-pity, or simply give up. That doesn't mean you've failed to forgive; it's simply that forgiveness is a process. You have to make daily, even moment-by-moment decisions to turn from bitterness and self-protection and turn to God. As you persevere, you will find it easier and easier to do. Don't complicate matters by insisting on a dramatic forgiveness experience. Let God's work unfold in your heart over time.

Remember That Jesus Makes All Things New

You may think if your marriage survives, it will always be a damaged, second-class relationship. This is not true. All marriages are damaged in one way or another. A marriage becomes beautiful when the husband and wife face their brokenness and invite Jesus to work in them.

In Paul's letter to the Ephesians, he prays that they would understand the hope they have as Christians. He explains that their hope rests on having the same Spirit of power that raised Jesus from the dead (Ephesians 1:18–20). This resurrection power guarantees your future eternal life, and also means you have a whole new life right now. Paul goes on to say, "As for you, you were dead in your transgressions and sins....But because of his great love for us, God, who is rich in mercy, made us alive with Christ even when we were dead in transgressions—it is by grace you have been saved" (Ephesians 2:1, 4–5).

The gospel of Jesus is about dead people and dead things being made alive; it is about renewal. Your marriage can be restored and become stronger and more beautiful as you persevere through this tragedy. The resurrection marriage isn't less beautiful because it has passed through death; it's more beautiful. It's a marriage that makes God's love, power, and grace visible to others. If you and your spouse persevere, your marriage can be glorious—a marriage made new by God's grace that is a living testimony to Jesus' resurrection.

Practical Strategies for Change

The pain of betrayal is like touching a hot stove. Your instinct is to move away—fast. You may be in so much pain right now that you can't imagine recovering and being able to trust your spouse again. You may feel that the quickest way through the pain is to end your marriage right now. Or you may feel the seductive pull of revenge. You want your spouse to get a dose of his or her own medicine: You want your spouse to be exposed publicly and to experience painful consequences.

Slow Down!

Let me urge you to slow down. The way you respond and the decisions you make now will affect you and your family for the rest of your life. You are in no state to make hasty decisions. After all of the time and effort you've put into your marriage, doesn't it deserve a few more weeks or months to make sure you've done everything you can? You don't want to live with regret and the feeling that you could have (or should have) done more to save your marriage.

Look for Counsel

Right now you need good counsel. You need people who love God to help you know the difference between hasty decisions and wise ones. You should move slowly in consultation with a wise pastor or counselor who has experience in navigating these treacherous waters. Start with your church community. More than likely your church leadership has had to walk others down this same path. They may be able to counsel you or refer you to an experienced counselor as well as activate a network of support for you within the church.

Set Boundaries for Your Spouse

Depending on the nature of your spouse's adultery, it could take some time for him or her to make a clean break from the relationship. Your spouse's willingness to end the relationship may vary from day to day, particularly if he or she was involved in a long-lasting relationship. Your spouse may be trying to keep you and the adulterous partner. It's very important for you not to get caught up in these shifting allegiances.

Your spouse needs to know that, for your marriage to get better, the adulterous relationship must be cut off. Indecision in this matter is a decision against your marriage. Until your spouse has made a real commitment to end communication with the other person, the uncertainty of your marriage should be reflected in the home.

So it may be appropriate for there to be some level of separation. It may be appropriate for you to sleep in separate rooms, or for your spouse to move out of the home altogether. It may be appropriate to refuse romantic overtures, dinners, or even sexual intimacy until your spouse has recommitted to the marriage. How to set up these boundaries depends on the individual nature of each marriage and requires a lot of wisdom. You should make all these decisions with the counsel of the trusted and wise people who are helping you.

Examine Yourself

Adultery is more likely to happen when a marriage is already weak. You should *not* take responsibility for your spouse's sin, but you may need to examine yourself and acknowledge how you contributed to weaknesses in your marriage. For some, the idea of examining yourself for failure at this point sounds unbearable, even cruel, but this is one way for you to stay connected to God's greater purposes for your life.

God will not let you be destroyed by this trial: Nothing can separate you from his love (Romans

8:28–39). God's plan is to use this trial to grow and strengthen your faith. Our hearts are always exposed by the trials in our lives. Now is a good time to see what is in your heart and ask God to forgive you. Your self-examination will bring an atmosphere of humility, honesty, and grace to your home, and it will remind you and your spouse that God is present and active.

Don't Take Responsibility for the Adultery

As you examine yourself, don't fall into the temptation of taking full responsibility for your spouse's adultery. Taking all of the responsibility usually has more to do with your fears than a genuine repentance. Confessing failure to your spouse to keep him or her from leaving you is manipulation. Instead of helping to rebuild your relationship, that kind of manipulation will have the opposite effect. This isn't a time for angry pride *or* fearful groveling, but a time to look to the Lord for faith and wisdom.

Remember, when we ask for wisdom, God will give it to us as we ask in faith (James 1:5–6). Look for ways your marriage could be better than it was before. Let your spouse know you aren't asking for a return to the status quo, but for an opportunity for the Lord to make your marriage better.

Talk about What Happened

For you and your spouse to rebuild your relationship, there must be a willingness on both of your parts to do the hard work of talking through what happened. Your spouse might want to avoid the shame and embarrassment of talking about the adultery, but neither of you can know forgiveness if silence surrounds the adultery.

Forgiveness is an important part of recovering from adultery, but forgiveness isn't God's way of "dropping the subject." When we confess our sins to God and ask for forgiveness, we are forgiven in an amazing way. Even these beautiful words from Psalm 103 can hardly express how complete God's forgiveness is: "For as high as the heavens are above the earth, so great is his love for those who fear him; as far as the east is from the west, so far has he removed our transgressions from us" (Psalm 103:11–12).

But God's forgiveness isn't a way for us to get off the hook; it's the beginning of building an intimate relationship with him. The Bible uses powerful images to depict the *result* of this forgiveness. One image is that of a wedding, two people becoming one. Another is adoption, an orphan brought into a loving relationship with a father. God doesn't forgive us and then walk away. God's forgiveness leads to real reconciliation. God's forgiveness draws us into closer relationship.

So you can't take the issue of your spouse's adultery off the table before the real work of healing and reconciliation takes place. For your marriage to become better, you have to honestly talk about what happened and why. A simple word picture may help. Ask your spouse to think of what happened as a painful and dangerous injury.

Probing and cleaning the injury might be painful and frightening, but wounds that are ignored or covered up don't heal well. You don't want to cover up an infection that could kill you. Begin by asking God to reveal all of the things that you and your spouse need to know to recover from this. In the same way that the adultery itself was revealed, ask God to reveal to your spouse the need to come clean about what happened and why it happened. Ask God to reveal the underlying or hidden issues in your marriage that made it vulnerable to adultery. Ask God to show you how he wants you to grow through this.

Reassure your spouse of your love and explain that you don't want to just survive what has happened—you want your marriage to be stronger. (To really mean this may take considerable prayer as well.) Let your spouse know you aren't interested in dealing out more hurt or shame, but in a better marriage.

Don't try to do this alone. It would be wise to

bring a third party into the healing process. Ask the pastor or marriage counselor who is working with you to meet with both of you on a regular basis to help you through this process.

Ask the Right Questions

As you talk through the adultery, it's okay to ask your spouse questions about the affair, but you need to ask yourself a question first: What's the point of my questions?

There are some good reasons to ask questions. It's important that there be no hidden issues that will emerge in a hurtful way later or be a source of guilt, shame, or bitterness in your marriage. You do need a full understanding of how you have been sinned against—for your forgiveness to be complete, your spouse's confession needs to be complete.

But there are also some bad reasons to ask questions. Sometimes after a traumatic event we become desperate to feel secure and in control again. We believe that, if we were more alert and had enough information, we could keep ourselves from being hurt again. You might believe that if you know enough about your spouse's sin you could master it and be able to protect yourself in the future. Of course, a complete knowledge of your spouse's sin will not protect you. Instead of relying on getting all your questions answered, you need to turn your attention to relying on God. Only he is your "ever-present help in trouble" (Psalm 46:1).

What kind of questions should you ask? It is appropriate to know the extent of the relationship: Were/are they "in love"? Was there a real emotional attachment or was it primarily sexual? How long has it been going on? If it was sexual, how many times were they together? As a rule of thumb, getting the general facts is important, but any details that make the adultery vivid make recovery difficult. Sharing details about sexual behavior is very destructive. These details create images that intrude at the worst possible moments and are remarkably persistent.

On the other hand, there shouldn't be hidden information that will surface later and create new wounds. For instance, if your spouse and the other person were seen together publicly (perhaps at a restaurant or on a trip), you should hear this from your spouse, not someone else. If money was spent on gifts, you should hear this from your spouse instead of discovering it when you look at your credit card or banking statements.

Ask these questions: What do I need to know that will help me work through the process of forgiveness? And what do I need to know that will help me entrust myself to God? If you are looking to regain your sense of control and security by knowing every detail of your spouse's affair, then it will be very difficult to stop asking questions. It's only as you entrust yourself, your spouse, and your marriage into God's care that you will be able to move forward after such a hurtful experience. Look to the Psalms to help you express the anguish you feel, and use them as your prayers. Psalm 34 says, "The righteous cry out, and the LORD hears them; he delivers them from all their troubles. The Lord is close to the brokenhearted and saves those who are crushed in spirit" (Psalm 34:17–18). Take this promise as your own. As you learn to trust the God who hears you and delivers you, your need to keep going over the details of your spouse's adultery will gradually end.

Recovering from adultery is a long, difficult road. To stay the course you will need daily encouragement and hope. You will need the support of godly and wise friends who will encourage you, pray with you and for you, and be available to listen to you. But most of all you will need to meet daily with Jesus, the one who makes all things new.